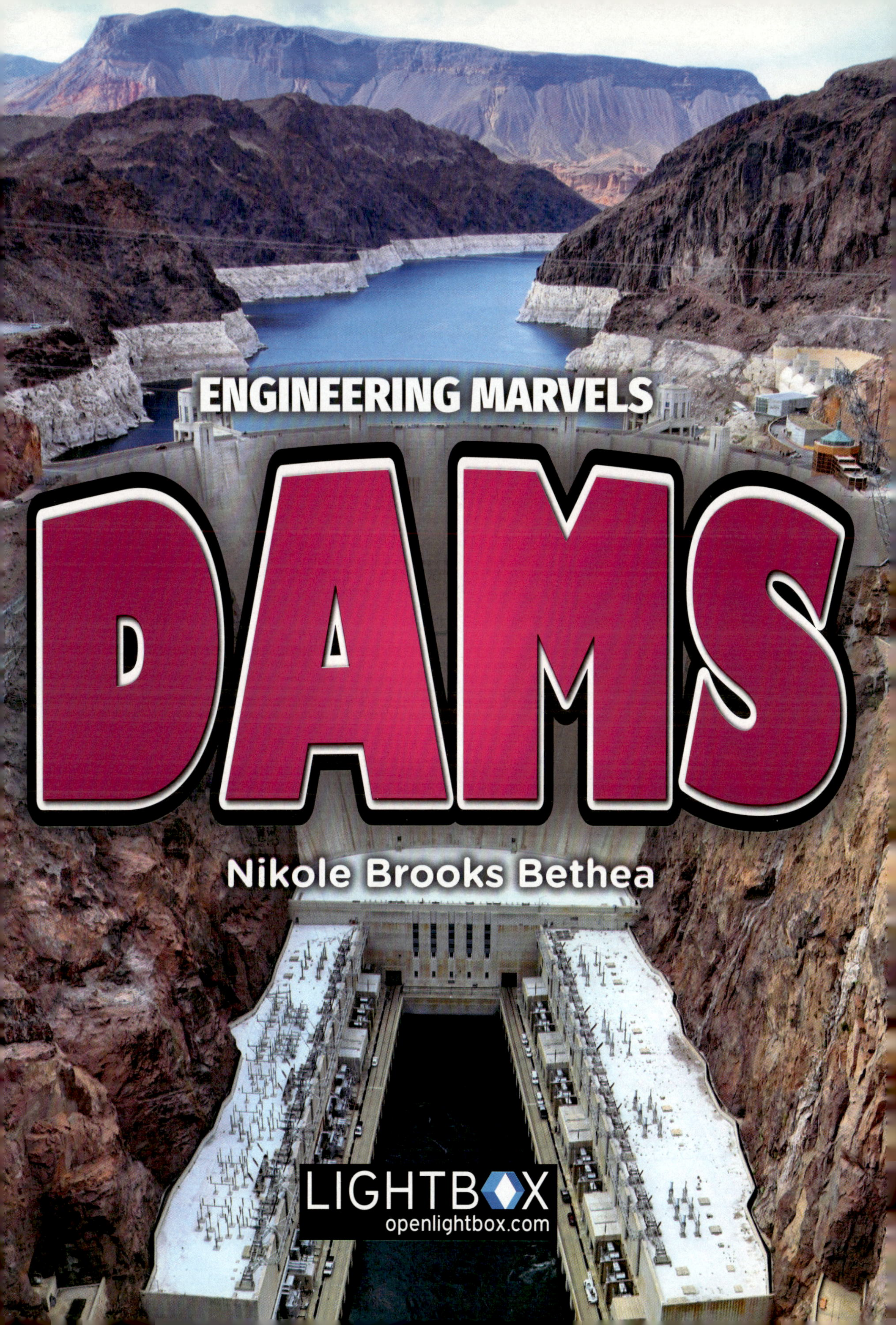

ENGINEERING MARVELS

DAMS

Nikole Brooks Bethea

LIGHTBOX
openlightbox.com

LIGHTBOX

Go to
www.openlightbox.com
and enter this book's
unique code.

ACCESS CODE

LBH59794

Lightbox is an all-inclusive digital solution for the teaching and learning of curriculum topics in an original, groundbreaking way. Lightbox is based on National Curriculum Standards.

STANDARD FEATURES OF LIGHTBOX

AUDIO High-quality narration using text-to-speech system

ACTIVITIES Printable PDFs that can be emailed and graded

SLIDESHOWS Pictorial overviews of key concepts

VIDEOS Embedded high-definition video clips

WEBLINKS Curated links to external, child-safe resources

TRANSPARENCIES Step-by-step layering of maps, diagrams, charts, and timelines

INTERACTIVE MAPS Interactive maps and aerial satellite imagery

QUIZZES Ten multiple choice questions that are automatically graded and emailed for teacher assessment

KEY WORDS Matching key concepts to their definitions

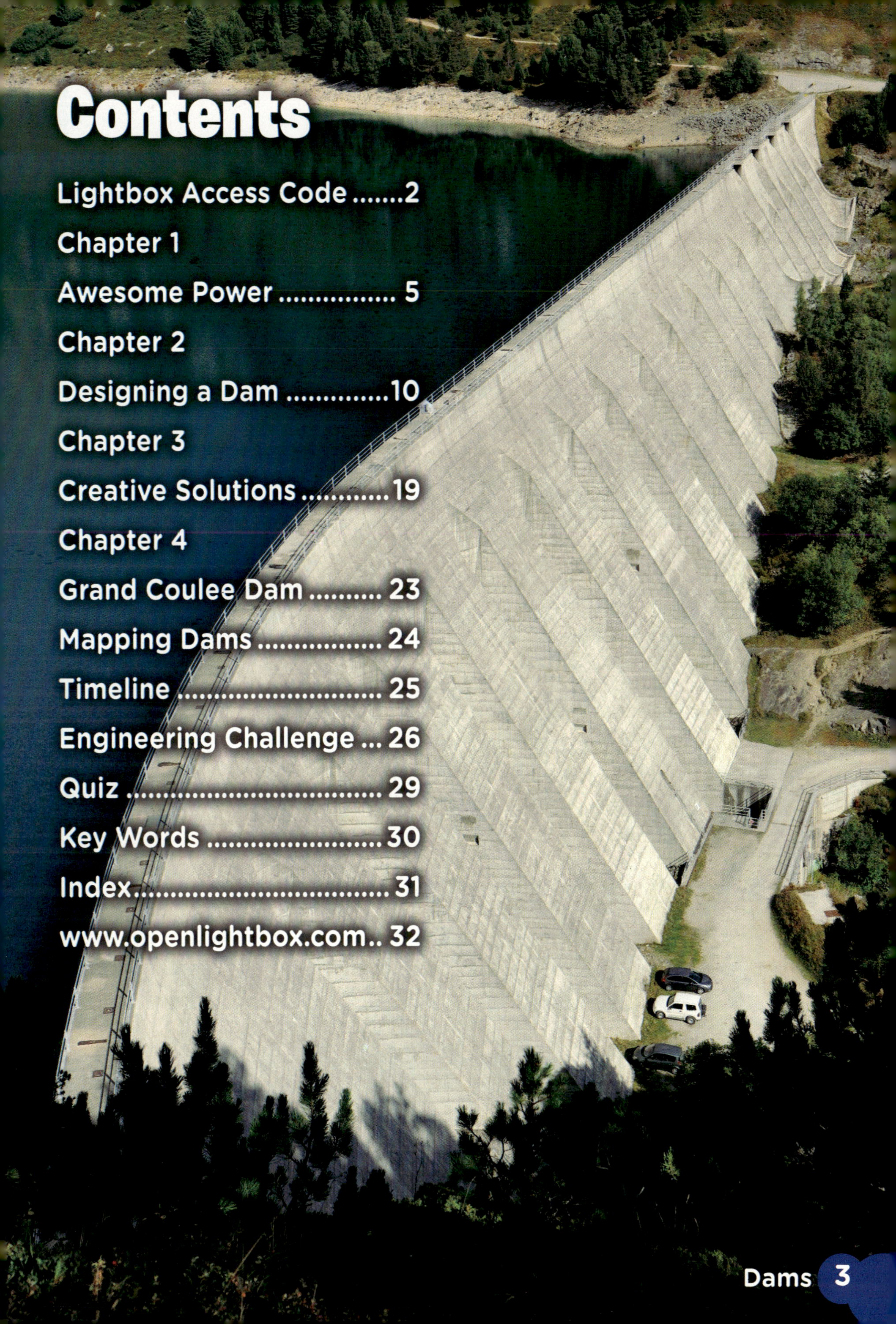

Contents

Chapter 1

Awesome Power

Han stood in awe in front of the Three Gorges Dam in China. The dam was more than 600 feet (183 meters) tall. It was more than 1.3 miles (2.1 kilometers) long. Powerful floodwaters emerged from the dam. Most impressive, though, was the dam's ability to **generate** energy. It is the largest **hydroelectric** plant in the world.

The Three Gorges Dam spans the Yangtze River in central China.

Water is necessary for people to survive, and people have always tried to control it. Dams achieve this goal. They are built across a river or stream to block the flow of water. This creates a **reservoir** behind the dam.

Outlets allow people to release the water downstream in a controlled way. This water might be needed for crop **irrigation** or drinking water. Or it might simply supply downstream flow.

One of the earliest dams was built in ancient Egypt around 3000 BCE. The dam protected the capital city from the Nile River's flooding. The Roman Empire also built dams. Two of them are still used today. Both are in Spain. They were built during the first and second centuries CE.

The ancient Romans built the 40-foot (12-m) Proserpina Dam in Spain.

About 850,000 dams can be found around the world.

One of the oldest dams still in use was built in Greece in 1260 BCE.

The world's largest beaver dam is 2,790 feet (850 m) long and can be seen from space.

About 7 percent of the electricity produced in the United States comes from hydroelectric power.

In the past, people built dams for flood control and irrigation. Ancient Roman dams had openings at the bottom. These released floodwater downstream.

The dams also had gates that could be opened. This supplied irrigation water from the reservoir.

Many ancient dams lacked **spillways**. Therefore, when water flowed over the top of the dams during large floods, the dams often failed. Modern dam designs include spillways. They allow large volumes of floodwater to pass over the dam or bypass it. This keeps the dam structure from being damaged.

Today, most dams are designed so they can generate energy. This is known as hydroelectric energy. The process begins when water reaches an area at the bottom of a dam. Flowing water has a lot of power. This water turns the blades of a turbine. The turbine shaft extends into a generator, causing it to spin. The generator produces electricity.

Chapter 2

Designing a Dam

There are two basic types of dams: **concrete** dams and earthen dams. Concrete dams can be arch dams, gravity dams, buttress dams, or a combination. Earthen dams are large walls of earth or stone called **embankments**. Each type has a different design. And each type of dam can serve a different purpose.

An arch dam is curved. The arched shape resists the force of water pushing on the dam. Arch dams are thinner than other types of dams. Therefore, less material is required to build them.

Water can flow through the Aldeadávila Dam in Spain at 410,000 cubic feet (11,700 m^3) per second.

Gravity dams stop the flow of water with their own weight. These massive dams are expensive to build. That's because they use large amounts of concrete.

Buttress dams are gravity dams with supports called buttresses. They can have a flat or curved face. Triangular supports are spaced along the back, or downstream side, of buttress dams. There are open spaces between the buttresses. As a result, these dams use less material than gravity dams.

Earthen dams are constructed of natural materials such as earth or rock. They often have a center core that is waterproof. The core might be made of clay or concrete. This prevents water from passing through the dam. These dams hold back water with their own weight.

Buttresses help support the Roselend Dam in France.

Dam engineers must consider many factors. First, they must decide what type of dam to build. **Topography** is the main factor that determines this. A stream running through a deep canyon with rocky walls requires a different design than a stream flowing through low, rolling hills. The geology of the site also determines the type of dam that can be built. The rock and soil must provide a good **foundation** for the dam.

During the design process, engineers study the forces acting on the dam. A dam must withstand the pressure the water applies on its upstream face. Dams must also withstand uplift pressure. This is an upward pressure from water seeping into the dam's openings and into the joint between the dam and its foundation. Engineers must also calculate how temperature changes will affect the dam.

The Katse Dam stands 607 feet (185 m) tall. It is the second-largest dam in Africa.

For example, water grows bigger when it turns to ice. Plus, engineers must consider the weight of the dam itself.

In addition, engineers must think about environmental and **ecological** changes that dams can cause. For instance, how will the change from flowing water to standing water affect the local wildlife?

The National Environmental Policy Act was signed into law in 1970. It requires engineers to consider environmental impacts when planning dams.

Engineering Design Process

Engineers must be confident in their plans. They use various codes, models, and tools in their planning. This ensures a dam will be strong enough.

ASK What type of dam should be built at this location?

IMAGINE Brainstorm the positive and negative aspects of each type of dam. How strong is the dam? How will it affect the environment? Choose the best type for this location.

PLAN Draw a diagram of the selected dam design. Write a list of materials needed.

CREATE Develop a computer model of the dam design. Input relevant forces, flood stages of the river, and rainfall data.

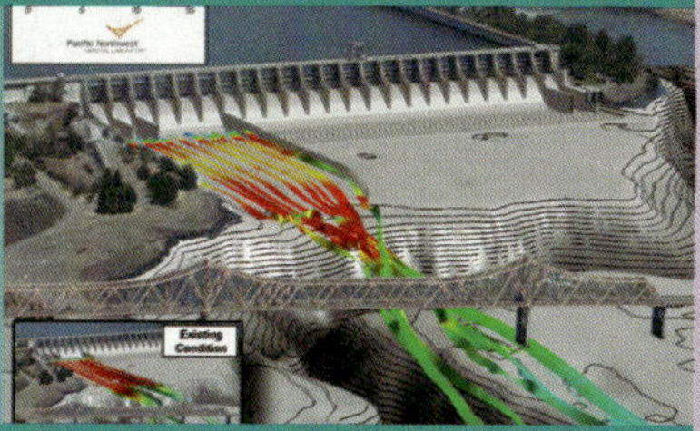

IMPROVE What worked? What didn't work? Modify the design and retest.

Chapter 3

Creative Solutions

The Hoover Dam is a giant concrete arch-gravity dam on the border between Nevada and Arizona. Building it was a huge, complex job. Before the first concrete could be poured, the site had to be dry. That meant the entire flow of the Colorado River had to be routed around the construction site.

Hoover Dam is a National Historic Landmark. It receives about 7 million visitors each year, more than any other dam in the world.

Engineers blasted four large tunnels through the canyon walls. Drilling rigs made holes in the rock face. Workers then filled the holes with dynamite and blasted. One ton (907 kilograms) of dynamite was fired for every 14 feet (4.3 m) of tunnel. The tunnels were completed in November 1932. Then, workers dumped rock and earth into the river to block its flow. The river began flowing through the four tunnels.

Engineers faced another challenge. Heat is produced as concrete is mixed. The concrete shrinks and cracks as it cools. Hoover Dam was to be 726 feet (221 m) tall. It would be 660 feet (201 m) thick at the base and 45 feet (13.7 m) thick at the top. All of this concrete would take 125 years to cool if poured all together. So engineers poured it into small blocks. Then, they placed pipes within the blocks. Cold water ran through the pipes to cool the concrete. Hoover Dam was completed in March 1936.

The original name of the Hoover Dam was Boulder Dam. It was changed in 1947 in honor of President Herbert Hoover.

Chapter 4

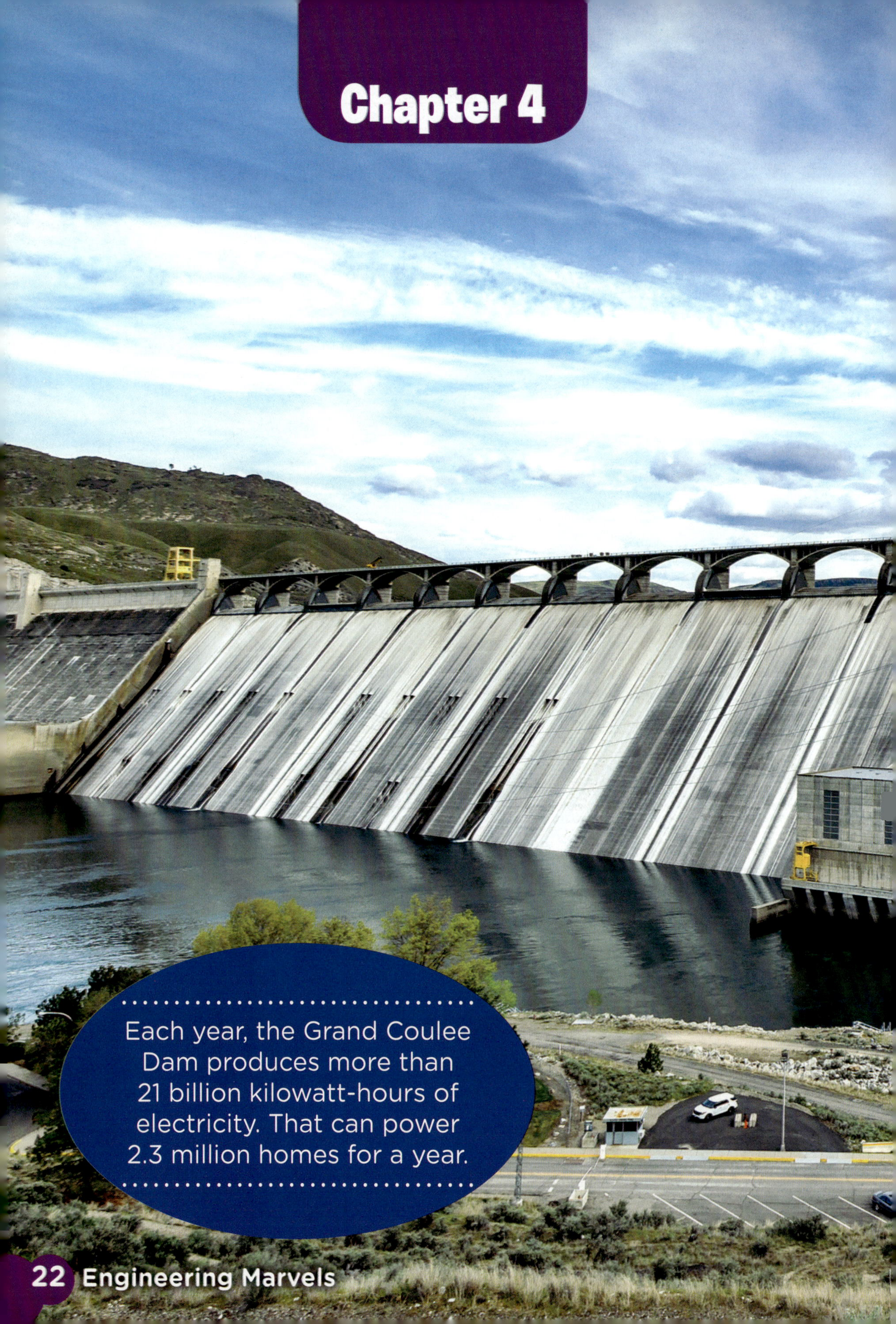

Each year, the Grand Coulee Dam produces more than 21 billion kilowatt-hours of electricity. That can power 2.3 million homes for a year.

Grand Coulee Dam

Grand Coulee Dam was finished in 1941 on the Columbia River in Washington. The gravity dam created Lake Roosevelt. At 550 feet (168 m) high and 5,223 feet (1,592 m) long, the dam is the largest concrete structure and the largest hydroelectric producer in the United States. It contains nearly 12 million cubic yards (9.2 million m^3) of concrete. That's enough to build a highway from Seattle, Washington, to Miami, Florida. In addition to producing electricity, the Grand Coulee Dam helps with irrigation and flood control.

Mapping Dams

The United States has some of the largest and best-known dams in the world. The map shows where a few of these engineering marvels are found. Are there any dams near where you live?

Dworshak Dam

Orofino, Idaho

Height: 717 feet (219 m)
Length: 3,287 feet (1,002 m)

The Dworshak Dam on the Clearwater River of Idaho is the third tallest dam in the country. The dam generates electricity and provides flood control.

Oroville Dam

Oroville, California

Height: 770.5 feet (235 m)
Length: 6,920 feet (2,109 m)

The Oroville Dam was built in the 1960s to support farming in California. It remains the tallest dam in the country.

Cochiti Dam

Cochiti Pueblo, New Mexico

Height: 251 feet (77 m)
Length: 5.5 miles (8.9 km)

The Cochiti Dam may not be very tall, but it is one of the longest dams in the world. The earthen dam stretches for more than 5 miles (8 km) across the Rio Grande River.

Timeline

Today, many large rivers in the United States have dams. They provide electricity, irrigation, and flood control to people across the nation. Discover more about the history of dams in the United States.

1882

The world's first hydroelectric power plant begins producing power. The plant dams the Fox River in Appleton, Wisconsin.

1902

The Bureau of Reclamation is created by the U.S. Congress. The bureau goes on to build more than 600 dams and reservoirs across the nation.

1960s

The United States reaches its peak of construction for large dams. The number of dams on rivers and waterways more than doubles, going from 9,687 in 1961 to 25,716 in 1970.

1980s

As the construction of dams slows down in the United States, it picks up around the world. Many dams are built in Canada, Russia, Brazil, and China, among many other countries.

2014

The largest dam removal project in U.S. history is completed. Two unused dams are removed from the Elwha River in Washington state.

2017

About 10 percent of the electricity used in the United States is generated from renewable sources, including hydroelectric power.

Engineering Challenge

In this activity, you become the engineer. You will construct a dam in the corner of an aluminum pan.

Materials

You'll need a baking pan, a cup of water, and materials to build a dam. Options include modeling clay, craft sticks, and rocks or gravel.

Procedure

Pretend a river is coming in from the corner of the pan. Without a proper dam, the river will flood the whole pan. It's your job to build a corner dam that will hold the water back.

1. Consider the four different dam types: gravity, buttress, embankment, and arch. Which one will be the simplest to make?
2. Use your materials to build the dam. Modeling clay works well for a simple embankment dam. Make sure to put the clay in a strong shape. Seal all the holes.
3. Pour water into the corner of the pan. What happened? Was your dam able to hold back the water?

Improve It!

How did your materials hold up? Could they be more effective if you used them differently?

- Pour out the water and dry the pan. Recreate your dam using different materials. Test it out. Does it hold better or worse than the first design? Are there ways you could make your dam even stronger by combining different types of dams? For example, you could add an arch shape. What about adding buttresses to strengthen your dam?
- Pour out the water and keep trying. See how tall you can build a dam without it leaking into the center area.

Quiz

1 Where is the largest hydroelectric plant in the world located?

2 When were the earliest dams built?

3 In the past, why did people build dams?

4 What are most dams today designed to do?

5 What main factor determines what type of dam is built?

6 When was the Hoover Dam completed?

7 Where is the Grand Coulee Dam located?

8 How many countries depend on dams for flood control?

9 When did the world's first hydroelectric power plant begin producing power?

10 When did dam construction peak in the United States?

Answers

1. China **2.** 3000 BCE **3.** Flood control and irrigation
4. Generate energy **5.** Topography **6.** March 1936
7. Columbia River, Washington **8.** At least 70 **9.** 1882 **10.** The 1960s

Key Words

concrete: a strong, stone-like material made from gravel, sand, cement, and water

ecological: relating to the relationship between living organisms and their environment

embankments: walls of earth or stone

foundation: the supporting base of a structure

generate: to make something new or cause something new to be made

hydroelectric: relating to the generation of electricity with flowing water

irrigation: the redirecting of water to help crops grow

reservoir: a human-made lake used for water supply storage

spillways: passages for excess water from a dam

topography: the features of the Earth's surface

Index

LIGHTBOX

SUPPLEMENTARY RESOURCES

Click on the plus icon found in the bottom left corner of each spread to open additional teacher resources.

- Download and print the book's quizzes and activities
- Access curriculum correlations
- Explore additional web applications that enhance the Lightbox experience

LIGHTBOX DIGITAL TITLES
Packed full of integrated media

VIDEOS

INTERACTIVE MAPS
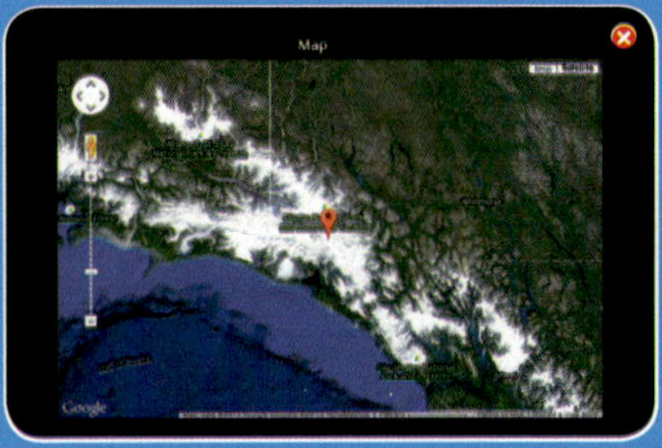

WEBLINKS
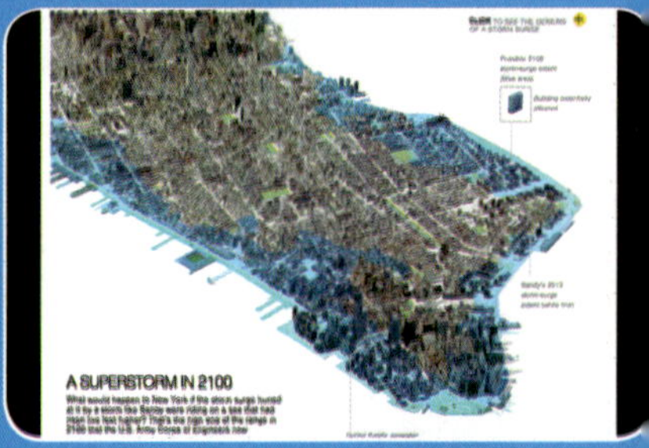

SLIDESHOWS

QUIZZES
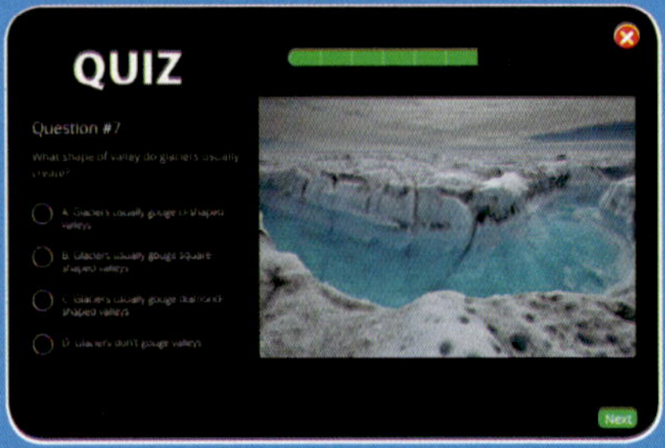

OPTIMIZED FOR
- ✓ TABLETS
- ✓ WHITEBOARDS
- ✓ COMPUTERS
- ✓ AND MUCH MORE!

Published by Smartbook Media Inc.
350 5th Avenue, 59th Floor New York, NY 10118
Website: www.openlightbox.com

012018
151217

Library of Congress Control Number: 2017961990

ISBN 978-1-5105-3728-6 (hardcover)
ISBN 978-1-5105-3729-3 (multi-user eBook)

Printed in the Brainerd, Minnesota, United States
1 2 3 4 5 6 7 8 9 0 22 21 20 19 18

First published by North Star Editions in 2018.

Project Coordinator: Jared Siemens
Designer: Ana María Vidal

Every reasonable effort has been made to trace ownership and to obtain permission to reprint copyright material. The publisher would be pleased to have any errors or omissions brought to its attention so that they may be corrected in subsequent printings.

The publisher acknowledges Alamy, Getty Images, iStock, and Shutterstock as the primary image suppliers for this title.